Finding 5% of My Life

A short story by Eric J. Nekich

PublishAmerica
Baltimore

© 2009 by Eric J. Nekich.
All rights reserved. No part of this book may be reproduced, stored in a retrieval system or transmitted in any form or by any means without the prior written permission of the publishers, except by a reviewer who may quote brief passages in a review to be printed in a newspaper, magazine or journal.

First printing

PublishAmerica has allowed this work to remain exactly as the author intended, verbatim, without editorial input.

ISBN: 978-1-4489-2156-0
PUBLISHED BY PUBLISHAMERICA, LLLP
www.publishamerica.com
Baltimore

Printed in the United States of America

This book is dedicated to; Dad, Mom, John, Sara, Lisa, Liam, Bella, Joe, Addy, and Marley. I love you all dearly and without you my new life would not be possible. Also, a special thank you to Ed and all of the staff at the Lawrence Center.

1

5%. That's how minute they say problem is, 5%. Shocking, depressing, takes the wind right out of the old sails. When you're in the middle of a perfectly uplifting "hangover high" they throw 5 % your way. See, you've only been clean for about 50 hours, you feel great about your self, and have wonderful visions of all the great things you can accomplish with your new found sobriety/ motivation. You don't think about the Librium in your system or the shots of thiamin in your ass that may have temporarily righted the ship. I mean the tongue isn't shaking so violently, you're not throwing up and you might actually be ready for a little food. You have conquered the one obstacle that kept you sick, broke, untrustworthy, unlovable, and unreliable; so, with it out of the way you are completely ready to take on the world again, like a twenty dollar quick oil change for your car, out with the old in with the new.

5%. You're playing out how great your life is going to be in your head like a made for TV movie and this guy hits the brakes. Ass. So he is basically telling you that your substance of choice; coke, grass, pills, booze, etc. is only 5% of the problem? That doesn't make any sense. That's a complete crock of shit. For over a decade that little annoying voice in your head has been telling you that once clean all would be grand in the world, and this shrink is telling you it's only 5% of the problem. *5%?* Just take a minute to try to wrap your head around *that*.

Wait, first take some pills designed to keep your body from going into a grand mall seizure. Combine them with a false sense of entitlement because minus those pills you've been substance free for at least two or three days. Move into a safe little place to live for awhile completely free of any temptation; then try to wrap your head around it.

Let me ask you something. Let's say you saw a sale sign that said 5% OFF!!!! Would you really give a shit? If you buy something for ninety nine cents and they tack on 5% sales tax and it is now one dollar and four cents, would you even think twice about your purchase?

Well, you might not believe me now, but 5% is what my life has boiled down to. It's the exact difference between life and *death*. Sound fucked up? It is. When you put yourself in a situation where your entire existence comes down to that small of a percentage, it is. Almost like a doctor telling you that you have a rare form of cancer and only a 5% chance of living, only more complicated. If it were cancer, you'd take your treatment and hope for the best, but mostly it is out of your hands. Here the cure is completely in your hands only you don't know it. You know where to go, but not how to get there. Only, you really do know how to get there, you're just not sure you really want to go or ever really would or could get there even though right now you feel like you're already there. At least I felt like I was there until this shrink started this 5% nonsense. Damn him! Less then a week into being cured and it all comes down to this…*5%*.

2
ALWAYS FIGURED I'D BE
A ROCK STAR OR A COMEDIAN

"You are either going to the hospital with me or I am calling the cops!" my loving sister relayed as only immediate family can.

What a horrible end to a seemingly perfect day. I had my swerve on; started working on that soon after I took my son to school *and picked him up.* Had stayed inside the house and out of the shower all day. Still had plenty of sauce left in my stash to carry me through tonight and into tomorrow morning. *I'll need a car to get more in the morning.* Was staring down the barrel of some mighty fine take out pizza and now this shit!

He should not have fucking called her. So she shows up unannounced. *Dad called her because you were acting funny/ scary again.* Lately my rants had gone from bad to worse while intoxicated. From loud and obnoxious to violent and physical. She starts going through my shit without asking, *to busy trying to look sober to notice,* and just happens to find my stash. A lovely assortment of empty bottles hidden all over my bedroom. I worked hard on those hiding spots, too.

"Those are from like two weeks, I mean a month, or two months…" I believe was my barley audible, slightly slurred, maybe mumbled response. Honestly, I barely remember. *Busted, think fast. I GOT IT, quick, turn on the tears and make everyone feel sorry for you, hurry up.* Some serious academy-caliber acting followed, which brings us to the very first sentence of this chapter.

Cops or docs, that is the question. Cops or docs. As tough as I have tried to look at times, I had never been to jail and certainly did not want to start now. *Can't get to booze in jail. Go to the hospital and I could still finagle a way to fire it up in the morning, just try to get everyone off of my back. Hospital it is!* I have been through the hospitals' protocol before for substance abuse. Check the vitals, hand over some literature, maybe a lecture or two depending on the doctor's work load at that time, observation, and on your way! *Genius for choosing the hospital, we'll be drinking again soon, no need to fear the withdrawal process.*

After years of spinning every situation and playing every single person to get exactly what I wanted out of it or them, I was not at all prepared for the situations or people who didn't buy the brand of bullshit I was selling. So goes the story of the weightlifting, she-male nurse from the south, and a family that has finally reached the end of their rope.

* * *

I did not drink; in fact, I loathed alcohol until my 18th birthday. To tell the truth, I never needed it. Never was really blessed with many inhibitions. I also had a front row seat to the horrible things alcohol induced minds and hands can do to a family. Maybe I wanted to *experiment*; maybe I was curious, maybe it was nothing in particular that made me decide to take my first swig. Only one thing was for certain, I LOVED being drunk. Some don't believe it, but it happened that fast. Like jumping off a bridge, I was only flying for a little bit, and then I hit the ground hard. The problem is lying on the ground looking up at the bridge, trying to remember what it felt like to fly, all of a sudden twelve and a half years have gone by.

* * *

Other than a little surprise from a latex covered finger in my ass, so far the trip has been exactly what was expected. *How much longer, I will need a car in the morning.* I had received my first lecture from a security guard of all people on the wrongs of my ways. He had been assigned to prevent me from harming myself. I was now simply watching some basketball, lying in a bed, in a cold room, in an ass-less gown. Just killing time before my discharge. H*ow much longer? I could borrow the neighbor's car; I'll just tell him I need some cigs.* Then she walked into the room.

A southern accent in Wisconsin never made much sense to me, strictly based on climate. If my eyes had been closed I would have been attracted to the sexy drawl; unfortunately, even with a blood alcohol level near the point fours, there was no flame being lit here. She was short and stocky, and could obviously kick the shit out of me if she wanted to. *Schmooze on, the quicker she thinks you're a great guy the sooner we are out of here. Play the depression/ I just had a little to much/life is so hard/feel sorry for me/let me go home/you're such a smart nurse now I am going to change/ thanks for everything/I finally get it because of you card.* Her no-nonsense demeanor was a little troubling, to say the least.

It was busy in the emergency room, and she was doing a great job advertising the fact that a wise cracking yet seemingly sad and depressed drunkard was not among her top priorities. I am almost convinced that she may have been born with a natural hatred of me. The stethoscope was a bit colder, the needles a tad more dull.

Okay, there will be no schmoozing, all systems commit to anger mode! Liars don't ever like being called out onto the carpet. Her southern drawl cut like a knife when she said the one word no one with plans for the next day, *after I get the car I will have to find a more discreet place to buy my booze, can't have anyone in the family see me with it, also, I need a much better hiding spot at the house, or I could just keep it on me...* ever wants to hear, DETOX.

And that was it. My family had been in the room to hear her recommendation. No matter what I said I wasn't getting out of it. *On the way to DETOX I could say I needed to stop and get cigs, then pick up some hooch!* "No stopping," she said. "Otherwise we can have you escorted over by an ambulance, if you would prefer?" It's funny because even though I had absolutely no control over anything in my life at this point anyway, I still got extremely pissed off about having zero control over this situation.

Everyone has a point at which they lay down and give up. Maybe it was because I had just gotten all the rest in the hospital bed, or because I felt quasi sober or because some higher power just reached in and gave me the push, but I was ready to throw in the towel. For tonight anyway. DETOX here we come!

At this point all of my cocky and cynical inner thoughts seemed to temporarily cease. The quick thinking portion of my brain that kept me going for so long had nothing to say. *Okay this is it, time to sober up for awhile, all systems commit to fear mode.*

3
THE LONGEST FOUR-MINUTE CAR RIDE OF MY ENTIRE LIFE

Your heart rate increases to the point where you feel like your ticker is going to jump out of your chest. You're light headed, like you're about to pass out. Your knees go weak and then suddenly it feels like you're going to swallow your tongue. Deep breath, deep breath, FUCK I can't breath, *I can't breathe!* This is it, I'm going to die, my body is shaking, almost convulsing. *I can't breathe!* I need to get to my truck. Like a fish needs water I need to get to my truck and get the hell out of here.

The door slams open and I run to the truck as fast as my noodle legs and oxygen starvation will let me. It's early yet, I have only been at work for five brief minutes. I start the vehicle and speed away as if leaving the scene of a crime. No stop signs; just as fast as I can go, get home, get home, GET HOME. Shaking, dizzy, crying, scared shitless and disoriented I slam to a stop in the driveway almost smashing into my garage door. I jump out of the truck and dash up the stairs, get the key in, I must get inside.

Sprint straight for the couch. Curl up in a fetal position. Just like a scared child. Just like a scared baby. I know exactly what is wrong. My doctor doesn't, my family doesn't, and not even my closest friend knows that I have started having anxiety and panic attacks on a daily basis due to alcohol withdrawal. Only God and I know. Know that something deep within my body is broken. Eventually it will pass; lately they have been lasting longer. And tomorrow, like everyday, I will go through it all over again.

* * *

They give me the option of who is going to transport me from the hospital to the DETOX center. *Not dad, that fucker got you into this! Not sis, that nosey bitch got you into this! Not bro, that detached bastard wouldn't get off his ass to help! That leaves mom, good old reliable and extremely gullible mom! If any of them would let you grab some fun on the way it's her!* I choose to let my mother give me the short car ride over to the DETOX center.

"I need to stop and get some cigarettes," I gently say to my dear mother. *Now we're talking.*

"That's fine, but I'll go in and get them. You just wait in the car." Again, the fight had been stripped from me. The sheer will it takes to constantly connive my way into what I want is non existent at this moment.

My mother returns to the car with one pack of menthol cigs and a bottle of water. I pound the water the same way I was accustomed to guzzling most of my beverage intake, pack and open the grits. Mom hates it when I smoke in her car, but I am going to anyway. One last childish act of rebellion. *Fuck it, they make you do this, you smoke in the car. Even Steven. Fuckin' rebel.*

The car veers west on county highway X and we are on our way. I have some idea what lies ahead due to my previous experience in DETOX. Three squares, a hard cot in a cold room, foggy brain, achy body, neat little journal to write in, nurse check ins, doctor visits, pills, shots, and right about the time I get to leave a little bit of guilt and resentment will start to creep in. *If I time it correctly, I should be good and liquored up again before I have to deal with any serious painful reflection.*

"Is this it?" Mom asks. *How the fuck should I know? This is your master plan, you figure it out bitch.*

Truth be told I don't remember much being out here on highway X, so this most likely was *it*. A blue and white sign illuminated in the dark night. Like a bug light for addicts and the mentally ill. We hit the steep incline at the entrance and came upon a brown little building that seemed entirely too square. How ironic. Not a lot of cars in the parking lot confirms my inner fear that I am in fact one of a kind. The engine stops and I begin to experience the first anxiety attack I have ever had while under the influence.

Exit the car and take in the frigid night air. My mouth feels dry and my head aches. All I want to do is sleep, but again based on prior experience I am fully aware that there are approximately ten hours of paperwork and procedure lying ahead. The little voice inside my head knows that beyond those doors is a virtual desert. No comfort booze on me, I consider making a run for it. *There has to be a warm bar around here somewhere?* Even the bravest and most desperate explorers reconsider during January in Wisconsin. *Okay just ride it out, no withdrawal with the medication so just ride out the storm.* We moved toward the main entrance and my mother opens the door for me. I would like to be poetic and say that for the first time I saw the pain I was causing in her loving eyes and suddenly felt the desire to change, but I didn't. Fucking pissed, fucking tired and fucking cold. Those were the only three feelings being computed by this selfish, shallow excuse of a human being.

4
DEFINITELY NOT CHECKING IN AT THE RITZ

I shit you not, this lady was a mole and a hair net away from serving me reheated spaghetti in the high school cafeteria. What was with all the big homely women tonight? Has any of this happened? Did I get in an accident when I picked up my son from school all pissed up and die? Is this hell? That's it! This *is* hell; and if I am not there yet, then this evening must certainly be an indicator of what lies ahead if I don't change my ways. *Make sure you ask her when you'll be out. When can we get lit again? Also, remember on your last day, spit out the Librium, if they give it to you. You mix that shit with booze and we'll be in a damn coma.*

She introduces herself and tells me her name, but I don't comprehend. She's close enough now that I can see a shave of the chin and upper lip is definitely in order. She ushers mom and I into a side room but I hit the water fountain first, gulping like a fish again. We are directed to sit and as soon as my ass hits that chair I need to use my fingers to hold my eyelids open. *Those that say sobering up in jail is the worst should compare and contrast to sobering up in a clinical environment. I feel like hammered shit, the tired I was feeling is now giving way to a nauseous, fevered mess I often refer to as sobriety, or a hangover for the laymen.*

A stack of documents on the chipped wooden desk is being brought to my attention and a ball point pen is being shoved in my face. One after another, like a robot, not listening, not looking, just initialing and signing, signing and initialing. *It is fucking hot in here! Could they honestly be trying to cook the addiction out of me? More water, I am so thirsty and definitely need more water.* Something about privacy practice; sign it. Something about releasing something to my physician; sign it. Something about insurance; sign it. Something about who you want to have permission to visit you…

Then something hits me, and I instantly want to cry. It could be that I am tired and ill feeling, but I think I want to cry. *Who do I want to visit me? Who the fuck wants to visit me?*

* * *

The green felt on the new pool table was almost a neon color. For hours we just stayed down here shooting pool and drinking and I wouldn't want to be anywhere else in the world other than down here with my friends. I have been drinking more than anyone else of course, like usual. Something set me off and I don't know what exactly but I am pissed off big time. The new pool balls make wonderful projectile weapons as I hurl them around the room. I am screaming some hurtful, awful things at my best friend. At the top of my lungs screaming, with all of my drunken might hurling pool balls and f-bombs. I'm on the floor now. My head probably bounced off the concrete, but adrenaline and mass quantities of alcohol make a great painkiller. Holding me down, telling me to be quiet, blood now running down my face, calming down, breathing and mood stabilizing, what the hell just happened?

* * *

"I don't want my father to be able to visit." I mumbled. *He should not have called her; it was none of her fucking business. Besides, what kind of pussy picks a fight and then calls his daughter for back up. I should have popped him when I had the chance. Oh well, this will teach him! He'll try to visit and they'll kick his ass out of the parking lot. Ha! Take that!* "On second thought, he can visit if he wants," I retracted. *What if I need something and he is the only one I can get it from. The addicts mind is a wonderfully selfish and self preserving place.*

Sitting here trying to think of a list of people that would not be allowed to visit *me*. Like it's my decision to make after burning every bridge I have ever built in my entire life one drunken rant after another. *Adolf Hitler, the devil, the boogeyman, O.J. Simpson, Brian Urlacher, and hey, shot in the dark here but can we toss long term sobriety on the list?* 30 years on this planet and I can barely think of any friends that would want to visit me, let alone foes. Pathetic. See when I am juiced up I prefer to be alone. Strip away all of that liquid tough guy courage, and I am sitting here scared shitless at the thought of doing this alone. *Could I get two beds in my room with no roommate so my mommy can stay with me?*

After the brief inner struggle, no one is excluded from this party! That's right folks we are taking down the old velvet rope so COME ON IN!

"Okay, that's it for this step. I'll give you a few minutes to say goodbye to your mother, and then I'll take you back." She states.

I stare at my mom as blankly as possible and say thanks. See ya. Adios. I think I have really hurt her. I always thought that her eyes would be filled with shame, disappointment, or anger at what her middle child's life has amounted to. All I see is genuine, heartaching pain in her brown eyes. For a moment I feel horrible about it. *How the hell do you think I feel! You drag me into this. You drag me here! Why am I the only one in this fucking family who has to change! What? The rest of you are perfect?* But I mainly just want to sleep. I am wiped out. I just want one last cig and then some sleep. The sooner she gets out of here, the sooner I can get back there. Whatever the hell is *back there?*

The door closes and I lose sight of my mom. Again, alone in a world that never made much sense to me, not that I was ever sober enough in my adult years to try to make sense of it, but still…alone. *I need a cigarette and some sleep.*

5
...A THREE HOUR TOUR...

Welcome to the *back*. She-male number two kindly introduces me to the first normal looking woman I have seen all night. The on duty nurse. Again no name is comprehended. I do remember that she had a nice smile though. She allows me my cigarette, and I can already tell that we are going to be great pals. *Because she smiled at you or because she let you have your way?*

I slip out an exit onto a snow covered patio and light up. The first drag I take long and hard and can feel the heat and smoke enter my lungs. Hold it in for a second or two, and release a loud obnoxious exhale. I begin to notice just how cold it is out here at night and decide it is in my best interest to power smoke. I am finished in a flash and head back inside.

She is waiting for me. "Okay, Eric, now I am going to show you around!" I don't know exactly what time it is, only that it is very late or extremely early and she is way too fucking chipper. She must be good at this job. Still smiling like there is no other place she'd rather be then giving tours to addicts at this hour. We walk down a hallway and pass a cafeteria on the right. On the left I notice a board with a large header that says "Daily Group Activities." Just glancing at it I can tell the days are full, like you'd be lucky to squeeze in a piss.

She explains that during DETOX I am not required to attend any activities, but it is encouraged. Further down the hall lies a seating area with a T.V. set. Thinking about all the activities scheduled has me wondering when the hell anyone would have time to watch it. They should just get rid of the damn thing. *What if it is here strictly for show? To fool the outside world into thinking this is a good place to bring a family member? "This is where the patients watch television, eat ice cream, laugh and play scrabble!" when really we are all hooked up to electrodes in the back room and have our belts taken away so we don't try to hang our miserable selves.*

Further down the hall and here we go, the bed rooms! We hang a left down another hall and she informs me that my suite is located on the right, across from the group showers/bathroom and just down the hall from the nurse's station. *Quite the prime little piece of real estate I might add. Good location!* As she begins to run down a massive list of rules, times, and procedures my mind already has me snoozing away in a cozy little twin bed. Blah blah blah, yeah yeah yeah, yes I would love an extra blanket and pillow, yes I'll make sure and acknowledge you when you check in, uh huh, uh huh, uh huh, search me for contraband, sure, yup, got it, alright. *Must sleep, need sleep, must sleeeeeeeep.*

She throws me another one of those award winning smiles and the door closes behind her. *...sleep at last, sleep at last, good god almighty, sleep at last...* I strip down to my boxer shorts and can definitely smell what a day of drinking and complete lack of personal hygiene amounts to. I crawl into bed and soon realize that this place is colder than the hospital. *How do you get colder than a fucking hospital? Thank god for the extra blanket, I can set the* *damn thing on fire to warm my appendages.* I shut my eyes and wait for it, wait for it, *wait for it...*

Soon I realize that I have no chance of falling asleep. Not because of the cold, or the sick sobering up feeling. I can't sleep because a thought keeps pounding through my head. Over and over again the same question, *"How the hell did I wind up here?"*

6
HEY, WHAT DID YOU GUYS DO LAST NIGHT? DID YOU GO TO THAT THING?

I am not required to wake at any given time while in DETOX, *and you thought I wasn't listening to nurse smiley last night!* but I can't sleep and I will be damned if I am just going to lie in bed all day. Besides, I need some water, a shower, the taste of tooth paste to replace the taste of shit in my mouth, and to get a hold of one of those Benedict Arnolds to bring me some clothes. I put on my soiled duds and head for the door. As if I had just stepped in quicksand my movement slows at the door and I pause without turning the handle. *Who's out there? I look like crap, I smell, what the hell will they think of me? Maybe I should lie in bed all day?*

If not for the sudden urge to vomit, I would never leave my room. I dart across the hall and have some dry heaves for breakfast. I have gotten used to the dry heaves by now. I have had them practically every morning for almost a year. That's why I avoided breakfast. No sense wasting the food.

While in the middle of my morning ritual, a voice beckons from behind one of the many shower curtains, "You alright dude? You gonna be able to make it to group?" I don't answer.

The shower shut off and soon there is a toweled gentleman standing over me. *Tell him you have the flu or something so he doesn't think it's because you're a drunk.* I look up at him and mumble something. He has to be in his late teens or early twenties, medium build with long curly brown hair, one of those trendy sea shell necklaces, a shit eating grin and a cocky aura about him that reminds me of someone else I know all too well.

"Are you cool bro, you want me to get the nurse?" He asks.

"No, no I'm fine, just a little under the weather man." I respond.

"Yeah, aren't we all in here man, aren't we all." I'm not sure if he's asking me a question or making a statement. It doesn't matter I guess because his next recommendation significantly alters the next week of my life. *That's right, little Wisconsin, hippie, surfer dude with the grin would make a definite contribution.* "Dude, if you feel good enough to go to group, then you should definitely go to group. Otherwise the days just fuckin drag by around here. Sure you're alright man?"

"Yeah I'm fine, thanks." I stand up and ask, "What time does *group* start?"

"I think in like 10 or 15 minutes dude, you can check the board in the main hall, I gotta get dressed, but you should totally go man. I hope I see ya in there!" *Ah yes the activity board in the main hall from the tour last night; again, I remember.*

I rinse my mouth out and take a few pulls off of the old water fountain, then make my way to the main hall.

7 – 7:30 breakfast
7:30 – 7:45 free time
7:45 – 9:00 group

I stand there staring at the board pondering the kind gentleman's open invitation to attend the *group*. I need to make a few phone calls. I need to shower and brush my teeth but I really can't do that until some one brings me a tooth brush and some fucking clothes. *Just go hide in your room. What if someone you know is in there?*

Get as far away from the rest of these degenerates as you can! Get back to the room and figure out how you are going to get the fuck out of here! Then it occurs to me that there is no place to go. Anyone that matters already knows exactly where I am. Not even a seasoned veteran like me can bullshit his way out of that one. *"Hey Eric, I heard you were in DETOX or rehab or something?" "No no, you've got it all wrong; I was in Detroit and then Reno, on business."*

Suddenly I'm confronted with another pounding thought flowing through my noggin. Similar to last night's, slightly different. *What the hell do you really have to lose?*

7
WOULD EVERYBODY PLEASE FORM A CIRCLE

I enter the room and attempt to distance myself from the rest of the people wandering in for *group*. Keeping a safe distance will not only help quarantine my distinct odor, but also hopefully make me appear as invisible as possible. I am beginning to have serious second thoughts about the decision to enter this portion of the little square building. I make an effort to fix my gaze entirely at the floor so no one will get the idea that I intend to hold a conversation or contribute to this in any way. *I can't believe this carpet. It seems like they use the same carpet in all of these establishments. Does it come in some kind of a kit for building a place like this? As soft as the concrete below it, almost like they just painted the concrete to look like it was carpeted.* It's extremely warm in here with the morning sun beating through the window. Quite the difference from the ice chest I attempted to sleep in last night. Either way it is clear that it will be difficult to get comfortable here. Maybe that's the point, we addicts know how to take advantage, if it were too comfy, we would never want to leave and face the outside world again. *What the hell are you doing in here, back to the room as fast as you can get there!*

I'm attempting to stand up and bolt out before anyone notices I'm here when *group* suddenly started.

"I see we have someone new this morning, would you like to introduce yourself? Your name followed by your drug of choice please," says the short, barrel of a man with the tie at the head of the "u" shaped pattern of chairs. Suddenly all eyes are on me, especially the man in the tie's. His eyes pierce through me almost as though he already knows my name and drug of choice. *Of course, the paperwork last night, shit! If he already knows the truth, how do I bullshit him?* I have noticed that when the opportunity arises for me to be completely honest, even for the simplest of things, it's always next to impossible to *be* honest. Like a predisposition to sling shit.

"My name is Eric, and I drink." *Perfect, short and sweet, hopefully it will be enough to keep him at bay.*

Everyone in the room says "Hi Eric" in unison.

The man in the tie begins to squint at me, and places a pencil in his mouth. Like I am a puzzle he is trying to solve or something. He speaks. "Eric, do you think most people who simply drink wind up in the hospital, or in DETOX?"

Here we go! "No," I reply.

"So is it safe to say that you may do more than just drink?"

Shit! "I guess." *If I needed something I could usually weave together a pattern of lies and excuses that would flow from my mouth smooth as silk. Suddenly in this hot fucking room, with these itchy dirty fucking clothes, with this shit taste in my mouth, in front of these strangers, in front of this prick with the tie, I'm speechless.*

"So then how did you wind up here?" *Hello, I have already asked myself that and will let you know as soon as I know!* "Cause **you're** in DETOX, and **you** came here from a hospital. Any guess what the amount of alcohol in your blood was?"

I feel sick. "Not really." *Again with the short answers. Have I met my match?*

"High, really high. People have died with a level like that. Sound like someone who just drinks?" I attempt to answer but he cuts me off. "Look Eric, I know you don't have to be in group so I commend you for coming." *I throw a nasty glance at the shit eating surfer dude," you should totally check it out dude"…aw shut the hell up!* "We are going to move on but I want you, I want all of you to think about where you are. People who just drink, or smoke a little grass don't come here and certainly don't wind up in the hospital. Now, whether you care to admit it or not, you are here for one reason and one reason only, you have a substance abuse problem. Whether you're an alcoholic or a junkie does not matter. You are here because you are powerless over your drug of choice and your life is *unmanageable!*"

Just as fast as his glare fixes on me it's gone and on someone else. *Good riddance.* His words hit my insides like a branding iron. As if all of this is a giant wrecking machine ripping apart a stone wall of denial. From this point on I know I will never be able to get rid of this idea, this fact. That no matter how much I drink to numb it or how much I try to justify my behavior, from this point forward the truth is released inside me, I have a serious problem. *I'm a…* I am not normal, and I don't consume alcohol normally. *I'm a…* He is right, my life is shit, and it is because I drink too much. *I'm a…*

8
I'M A...

There is this scene in the movie Good Will Hunting where Robin Williams is asking Matt Damon what he wants to do with his life. Matt has no clue, and tells him he wants to be a shepherd. I never liked that scene. Up until this scene, Damon's character Will seems like a cool tough guy who knows exactly what he wants. During this scene you realize he is a clueless wise ass who can't fool everybody.

* * *

Try and imagine waking up in the morning in instant fear. Fear of alcohol withdrawal. If you have the day off it's no big deal because you just take your first drink before you even brush your teeth and you'll be fine. If you have to work and aren't blessed with the kind of profession that allows you to consume large quantities of alcohol, or simply can't get your hands on any sauce then sit tight because withdrawals are coming.

Whether you drink or not that morning, you are still going to be sick. Dry heaves usually for me because I rarely ate enough food for my body to have enough left over to toss back out. That's the part I hated because the first couple of drinks were always wasted and lets face it, I was a budget junkie.

Okay, now that the heaving and puking is over, you shower, and wait for the anxiety and panic to kick in. The tongue shakes are the worst. *At least in my experience.* Now, you're a drunken bastard without a pot to piss in or a window to throw it out of, so throughout the panic and anxiety you must panhandle within the family in order to get more booze because you would rather die than go too long without it. *On several occasions I have honestly thought I was minutes away from a grand mall seizure if I went more than twenty four hours without fifty drinks.* Try to remember your excuses and cycle them in accordingly. For instance, if you lied to your sister two days ago about needing lunch money for the kid, you need to wait at least a week before using that one again.

Cigarettes. That one is grand. If you smoke a half a pack a day, tell everyone you smoke a pack a day. Most times they will just hand you a five, which buys a pint of vodka, and you will have change left over towards more booze for tomorrow! If you use this method, be sure you ration out your smokes though. Going without booze is tough enough. Going without booze and cigarettes will have you ready to pull your fucking hair out.

If the family is pulling one of its stupid "don't give the drunk money" protests, remember, if you've got checks, you've got money. Who cares if it bounces to the moon, you don't think that far ahead.

Now as soon as you get the chance, before you do anything else, chug the shit right out of the bottle. Fuck ice, and fuck mixers, that shit is for frat boys and happy hour one drinkers. Time to get completely annihilated. We are going to drink until we don't remember a thing the next day. Drink until you pass out and piss your own pants. *If you do it enough you stop caring. Who cares if you pee your pants if you never have to share your bed with anyone.*

Now it's time to wake up and do it all again. Everyday of your life. Every second spent on or about alcohol. Whether it's figuring out how to get more or feeling the effects of too much for too long, it has become your entire life. Your entire life is wrapped up in a twenty four hour mission to get as drunk as possible, as often as possible. And when you're not, all you're doing is paying the price for it anyway, so you might as well do whatever it takes to just stay drunk.

* * *

When you have lived in as tiny a box as I have for as long as I have, it is next to impossible to think outside of it. I know I am an alcoholic at this point, but that one word doesn't seem to paint the picture and I do not yet understand its full meaning. A laundry list of horrible words and phrases come to my mind as I am now in a sudden state of self reflection, or is it self realization? I am...

Selfish
Stupid
A cheat
A liar
A coward
A sinner
A bad parent
A bad son
A bad brother
A horrible Christian
An idiot
A drinker
A thief

A waste
A complete waste
A manipulator
A bad seed
A black sheep
A criminal
A bad influence
A fucking waste.

I had forgotten where I was. When I finally realize it I excuse myself and run to my room as fast as possible. Run to the bed, curl up in the fetal position, scared shitless, I cry. I weep. I wail. *I am…not ready for this at all. I have no idea what it is I am not ready for, I only know I want no part of it.*

There is something about a complete stranger calling you out that sends you reeling. If I had been drinking, I would have argued with him, pleaded my case, and at least put up a little fight. But this was me sick and sober. See, I have been drunk for so long, that I don't know who I even am when sober. Other than the physical side effects of not drinking, the psychological side effects are just as bad if not worse. It's almost like I am just piloting this body that I borrowed for the day. The thirsty part of me uses the other part of me merely as a vessel. A fucking zombie. That's exactly what I am sober, a fucking zombie. In any scary movie, have you ever seen a zombie try to process emotion? Nope, no you haven't. They are always too busy roaming around and consuming people to ever take a few minutes and consider the effects of their course of action.

9
A ONE-LEGGED MAN IN AN ASS-KICKING CONTEST

I couldn't tell you the last time I set a goal in my life. *What about the daily goal you set to get booze and get smashed.* I can't tell you about any dreams or aspirations I ever had in the last twelve years. I never had time and my mind never allowed me to. It's like I was stuck in this weird mode of strictly surviving. Surviving only to drink. After that *group* session, a few things are very clear to me. That I do not like whom I have become, that I don't know how I got to this sad point in my life, and that I am really tired of it all.

Some would say that being fed up is a good thing for someone in my condition. That it's exactly what you need to be able to make a positive change in your life, and they would be right as long as the person making the change sees some hope or direction that there *will* be a **positive** change.

Here I am looking at all of these things, situations, and relationships in my life that are destroyed and need to be mended, if it's possible to even mend them. Here I am feeling sick, tired and scared. I want to go home, but I don't know where home is or even if I will be welcome any place I think might be a home. *Here I am. More like here it is. Do I even consider myself an "I" anymore? An "I" has a soul, I must just be an "it." Or, "it" must just be an "it," you get the fucking point.*

As the tears begin to subside, I rise from my bed and head towards the window. The snow looks beautiful with the sun shinning off of it. Glittering like a million tiny diamonds. *When is the last time I noticed anything like that? When is the last time I noticed anything at all?*

When the moment that may change your life occurs, you'll never know while it's happening. *Do I want to die? No dealing with the guilt, no more feeling sick, nothing to mend, just sleep and never wake up. Actually the act of suicide might mend these things on its own? Instead of people being pissed at me, they'll be sad I'm gone.*

Or will they? Who the fuck would miss me? Who the fuck would miss the shit you put them through? Do I really want to die? What would happen to my son if I died? It was that fast. The thought of making him sad or fucking his life up by committing suicide is gone as fast as it arrives and it could only mean one thing…that I want to live.

Now let's get down to the idea of a quality life. Even I, **Captain Denial**, know that what I have now is far from what anyone would call a life. It is a mess and a huge one at that. I honestly feel **completely** lost when sober, like I don't know what to else to do but drink. If my life couldn't revolve around drinking, then what the hell else was I supposed to do? What the hell am I going to do? Lost. Completely lost at thirty years of age. *Well what the hell does everyone else do? Apparently some people do what I do, that would explain the attendance at this morning's group. But what about everyone else? They have to do something right? Right?* So it is here when a few more things became clear to me. That I certainly do not want to die and that there has to be another way. To normal people that's common sense. To me it is like catching lightning in a bottle.

It's as though I am putting together a very small and very fragile foundation. If I am careful, I might just be able to build something off of it.

10
CATCHING LIGHTNING IN A BOTTLE AND ONLY BEING STRUCK A FEW TIMES

Addicts tend to be pretty much all or nothing people, *I don't want just one beer, I want one hundred beers. I don't want just one crack rock; I want the entire crack quarry.* And this is exactly why the next two days of DETOX completely fly by. *If I was going to be forced to be here, then I was going to make the most out of it. I was going to listen, read, write, say and do anything they told me to. I was all in, and upon discharge if I drank I could at least say that I tried, that I was simply allergic to their brand of medicine.*

In two days I put in some serious work, and start to put together some ideas in my head. Some *positive* ideas. I realize that the amount of effort it took to stay drunk on a daily basis was vast. No small feat indeed, to be that resourceful. *If I could apply half of the resourcefulness it took to stay drunk all those years to staying clean, I might just be okay.* It also occurs to me that there was no such thing as a mess too big to clean up. It certainly would not get clean in one day, and certainly not alone. *Look at what you destroyed all alone and imagine what could be built with some help.* That some situations and relationships will never be mended and that that is beyond my control. *Learn what the things are in your life that are beyond your control. Learn to let go. Learn to let go and let God.*

I learn that it is okay to be a human being, and that human beings make mistakes, and that this is only a mistake, a gigantic nasty mistake for everyone involved. This is an illness. A disease. A horrible disease, but still just a disease. *Keep in mind that at this point I have merely said that I have learned these things. I have yet to master the force and am still very much a young drunken Jedi.* I become an expert on addiction *"and with this knowledge he shall go forth and be clean."* I am cured. Healed. There is no way on earth I am ever drinking alcohol again.

I have daily visits with a doctor while in DETOX. The results from my blood work should be in today. I wonder how my liver and kidneys have reacted to the prolonged exposure to poison? I am honestly expecting the worst. Why should my internal organs react any differently than anything or anyone else after what I have put them through? *Screw you Eric, we fucking quit!*

"Everything looks pretty good. No long term damage yet. How are you feeling Eric? Hold out your hands please." *So he can see how bad they are or are not shaking.* "Alright, today we will start weaning you off of the Librium, but we are going to keep up with the thiamin and folic acid, not quite out of the dark yet." *Shit, that's right I have had happy pills in me this whole time! Could my uplifted state be chemically induced? Will I still feel cured post mind altering?* "One last thing, the front office wanted me to send you in when I was done with you, so head on up and I will check with you tomorrow morning."

I am pretty sure I am missing an activity with the group for this and I am kind of pissed about it. *That's a good thing! Pissed because you can't go to group? You went for the bait when you were weak and now you have fallen right into their trap!* Oh well. There will be more groups. No shortage of group activities around here, that's for sure.

"Hi, Eric?" *an attractive lady with a wonderful smile says. The staff here always seems to be smiling.* "Come on in and have a seat."

"What's up?" I say.

"Are you feeling better?" she asks with a genuine sense of concern.

"I feel great, I really do." I reply with a pretty genuine smile. Free of most of my usual cynicism.

"That's good to hear. So, okay, looks like after your last doctor's appointment tomorrow morning" *did she just say last?* "you are going to be discharged!" *Did she just say discharged?* "So, since tomorrow is Sunday, we need to get all of your paperwork ready today so after your appointment you will be free to leave!" *Now that smile isn't so nice. I'm leaving tomorrow? That's it? But I am just starting to...*

I can instantly feel my body temperature rise. My hands grow sweaty, my heart rate increases, my throat is suddenly thick, and my breathing becomes short and shallow. The positive mind set I was in is gone in a flash. *Okay, so the neighbor probably doesn't know where I am so I'll say I need cigs and borrow his car. There is a twenty dollar bill in my sock drawer at dads. I'll have to go there anyway. More than likely he won't say a fucking word to me. My sister is way too fucking nosey. Okay, we've got the car and the money; now, how do we conceal it this time and not get caught. GOT IT! I'll wear my thick work coat with the inside pocket. If dad says anything I'll just tell him I'm cold. Now, where to consume? Well, I'll have to do some laundry; in fact I can stash a bottle down there so when I am changing loads or folding I can pound some. Good idea, that way if anything happens to the shit on me I'll still have that one as back up. Bathroom, yes the bathroom! I can pound a bunch while I'm in the shower, and then I can just keep going in there and locking the door behind me while I drink! If the old man says anything I'll just tell him they gave some medication in here that makes me piss a lot. A diuretic, I think they're called. Buy as much as you can though. The fewer trips to the liquor store the better. Hiding spots? The garage, in the loft above the garage door. A lot of work to get a little booze, but I will be damned if anyone is going to find my shit this time. And whatever happens, no matter what is said I have to keep it cool this time. This time I have to look sober all the time or it's going to be this shit all over again. FUCK, is it tomorrow morning yet?*

I am safe and sober and changed for good as long as I stay locked in this little place. The very thought of freedom has me craving like a fiend. Forget cleaning up any mess, or letting go and letting *who*. This is not a disease; this is how I want to live. THIS IS WHAT I WANT. THIS IS ALL I FUCKING WANT!

11
WHAT DO YOU WANT TO DO WITH YOUR LIFE, WILL?

I just have to fake out the rest of this day and tomorrow morning. Check in with the doctor; say my goodbyes and I am out of here! *Remember not to take any Librium if he offers. And be sincere about not wanting to leave so they all think you're cured and there is no way in hell you will ever pick up another drink. Like shooting fish in a barrel, fooling these degenerate bastards will be like shooting fish in a barrel.*

Under the excitement of having my next drink, and the cloudy rapid movement of my rusty brain, *rusted from being off of my game for a few days,* I start to notice another emotion flopping around inside. It starts as a faint whisper and seems to be getting louder and louder inside my body.

It's not anger. I get to leave and drink. It feels like fifty butterflies have been let loose inside my stomach. *I'm not sad. I get to leave and DRINK.* It seems like it is getting harder to swallow? *I don't think it's a panic or anxiety attack; you still have the happy pills in your system.*

I am starting to worry. Worry about what? *Yeah, what the fuck would you worry about? WE GET TO LEAVE AND DRINK!*

I think I'm scared, I think I'm afraid, oh my god, I'm scared shitless? *Scared of what? Are you positive it's not just performance anxiety? Are you sure it's not excitement or anticipation? TOMORROW WE GET TO FUCKING DRINK!*

I'm scared of... I'm afraid of...I am scared shitless of me.

I'm scared of me. I'm scared of the voice inside my head. I'm afraid of leaving this place. I'm afraid to go back. I'm scared to walk right back in. I am scared shitless to walk, all alone, back into hell. And tomorrow, in the late morning or early afternoon, I know that is exactly where I am going to go, and there is no way I am going to talk myself out of it. All of the building bricks in my small and fragile foundation seem to be gone.

Did I ever really want to get sober? Did I ever really want to live a life without alcohol? Do I want to die? I must want to. I must want to die...

12
LET GO AND LET *WHO?*

Here is where the three most important words I have ever muttered fly out of my yapper. "I can't leave."

"Excuse me?" she says. She has been explaining some release forms to me and I have no idea. I am just stuck inside my thoughts as usual. Ignorant to all except the immediate inner workings of my often dangerous mind.

"I can't leave."

"Well, pending your doctor appointment, tomorrow is your scheduled discharge?" I could tell that I wasn't the only one in the room that was a little confused at this moment. "And besides, there is the matter of payment. I haven't heard back from your insurance provider, but if they won't cover any additional days you pretty much will have to leave." Suddenly the warm smile was replaced with an all business demeanor. "Unless, you can pay cash; however, it's expensive and you would still need a recommendation for inpatient treatment from either the doctor or one of the counselors." *You could stop now and say you tried; it's officially not your fault, you're off the hook just the way you like it baby. You could blame your relapse on the health care crisis in America!*

"How expensive?" I ask

"$770.00 a day. Depending on what the recommendation is, pending your insurance, you are required to pay for everything up front." She states. I can tell she is a bit saddened. *Or it's Saturday and she wants to get the hell out of here. You know; kind of the same place your head should be at right now!*

"Wow. That is expensive. I don't have that much. Maybe I'll figure something else out, thanks for your time." And I leave her office, confused. Confused, yet slightly determined. Apparently addicts have a natural resistance to the word "no."

* * *

"...So as soon as she told me I was leaving, I played this whole relapse out in my head. I mean everything, down to the last detail and it really scared me. It made me really think about why I'm here. There is no doubt in my mind, I leave tomorrow, I drink tomorrow." I am almost out of breath when I finish telling my story to the man in the tie. I have no idea how long I have been rambling. He just sat there all barrel chested and squinty eyed chewing on that pen.

"Two days ago you were only in here because you *drank*." Man this guy is blunt. "What changed? Why now do you *need* to be here so bad?"

"I think I understand that something is wrong. Something is really wrong. I mean, who the hell thinks like this? I just guess I want to stay clean a little longer, learn a little more, you know, take this in and give it an honest chance." *Speaking of honesty, where the fuck was all of this coming from. Barely one month into the New Year and I have already topped last year's high of honest things to come out of my mouth.* "I know that out there, right now, I won't get that opportunity. I know I'll instantly fall into my old habits, drink, and probably die. I don't want that, I at least want to fight a little you know. If I'm going to go down, I want to go down swinging." *This guy is a hard sell, or at least he's acting like one.*

"Alright, I'll make a recommendation on two conditions." *YES!* "First, you keep working as hard, if not harder, as you have been. I mean you best not miss one activity, you better do whatever is asked of you, got it? Second, you're going to have to come up with the money. I can't help you there." *YES!*

As I stand up and shake his hand, I realize that this is the closest I have remotely felt to happy in a long time. As I walk out I can feel myself glowing and the muscles in my cheeks hurt from the huge smile on my face. *Muscles hurt from smiling? Must not be used to being in that position. Haven't had many reasons to hold that position in awhile.*

"By the way Eric, it's addicts," he says as I am just about to round the corner.

Confused I reply, "What?"

"Addicts, Eric, addicts are the ones who think like that." It is hard to tell, but a tiny smirk appeared on his face, almost an evil smirk. Pleased that his master plan had come to fruition. *Of course they do. Addicts think like that, I think like that, I am...*

13
DOES ANYBODY HAVE A FEW EXTRA BUCKS?

This sudden motivation to stay here has me surprised. Approximately seventy two hours ago I was ready to sneak out the window into the cold January night, and today I am begging a counselor for a recommendation, and contemplating a very difficult phone call. A *key part of my existence has been trying to always fly under the radar. Avoid detection at all costs. By making this phone call, and being honest, the proverbial cat will forever be out of its bag.*

To this day if I could have gone anywhere else for the money I would have, and that makes absolutely no sense to me at all. I had borrowed money, *well I guess the right word isn't borrowed because every time I asked for money I knew I was probably not going to pay her back, I think she knew it too,* from my sister every other day now for about the past six months, predominately for hard liquor. For some reason I did not want to borrow it for this. *Because then you would be admitting to her your problem, and if down the road you ever changed your mind about staying sober, she would know the truth because this isn't DETOX anymore, she would have given you the money to go to rehab, and people who should be drinking have never been to rehab.*

I start to see it as asking for money to stay alive. I don't see the shame in that. If I leave I drink and I die. If you give me the money, I stay a little longer, *maybe* I don't drink, and *maybe* I don't die *at least quickly in a drunken car wreck or slowly from cirrhosis.* I haven't had a drink in awhile, I am almost through withdrawing, but the hand that is holding the phone is shaking violently. *Again with the fear.*

Just hang the phone up man. This isn't worth it, it shouldn't be this hard. Think Eric, if it were meant to be would it be this hard, or would it just happen. She's gonna yell at you, give you the "you only call when you need something" riot act. Let's just go home and we'll figure something else out. Here I was and my relationship with my only sister was so fucked *at least in my mind* that I was afraid to call her and ask her to help save my life. *Is there anyone else? Anyone?* No, there wasn't anyone else. No one I could think of with the resources to help, who might actually consider helping. *I really don't want to do this.*

Look, I know it probably seems melodramatic to make this much out of a phone call to a sibling to ask for money. But it is. And it brought another factor into this equation. A question I have read and can not answer. The question all addicts trying to get clean must ask themselves at one point or another. *Was I willing to do whatever it takes to get sober?*

14
I AM…

At this point I have been in inpatient rehabilitation for chemical dependency for almost a week, thanks to my sister shelling out thirty five hundred smackers so I could stay. *Did you think it was going to go the other way? Don't feel bad, I did too.* And here is what I have put together so far. I am…

An alcoholic
Sick
Diseased
A human being
A good person
A loving father
In need of help
In need of a change
Ready to change
Scared
A good Christian
A good brother
A good son
Optimistic

A good friend
Trustworthy
Reliable
Honest
Worth loving
None of the above when I use alcohol

"Okay guys, now I have a question for you. What percent of your problem is the alcohol or the drug itself? This is important so please participate. Let's start with Eric. How much of your problem is alcohol Eric?" The counselor asks. *At the time the correct answer could only be one thing right?*

"100%!" I respond with enough enthusiasm to make a high school pompom squad proud.

"So you feel that the alcohol is 100% of your problem?" he questions. *The chance he gave me here to re-answer should have set off a flag or two that I may be wrong.* Around the group he goes and one by one addicts shout out astronomical figures. From the bad arithmetic, "150%!" To the uncertain, "50%?" To extreme denial, "5%." Wait a minute, did *he* just say...

15
5%

5%? The counselor in charge of this session just informed us that the alcohol or the drugs were a lowly 5% of the problem? I am ready to jump out of my seat because it is clear that recent alcohol or drug intake has to be a percentage of his problem! 5%! That's nothing. *That's fucking nothing!* All the shit that I have been through, the whole reason I am in this room listening to this crack pot, *listening?* is because of alcohol! *Listening?* All of the financial problems, legal problems, health problems, people problems I am facing or have faced and all of that is 5%! *Listening?*

He is still talking and I am not *listening.* He is explaining himself, so I'd better *listen* so I understand because there has to be more to this, *or find out where he gets his weed.*

"The actual drug or alcohol itself is only 5% of the problem. The other 95% of the problem is the behavior. The attitude, the outlook, the patterns, the rituals, the people, the places. You can get rid of the 5%; but, if you don't address the other 95% of the issues that all addicts have, you will not experience anything close to long term, quality sobriety, period!"

It's a hard statistic to swallow. When you first get clean you really think the problem is solved simply by not consuming. You don't think about the mountain of change and the lifetime of commitment you face if you intend on staying sober. Here is where the ultimate question rears its ugly all important head. Are you ready to do whatever it takes?

I, for instance, have just been issued a clean bill of health, *strictly physically speaking,* I have actually had a chance to review some of the financial damage and it isn't as bad as what was first thought, and my family came to visit *and my sister funded this journey* so they must still love me. You would think you would count your blessings, be thankful things are still fixable, and move on with your life lesson learned. Unfortunately, that is not how this disease works, and you haven't been clean long enough or learned enough about your disease to understand that. You still see one last opportunity. One last crack left in the door large enough to slip through. With this clean slate part of you still thinks you can continue to use, and this time just keep it in check so it doesn't get *this* bad ever again. *A beer here or a beer there, a drink before bed. No more drinking in the morning, period. Maybe even no more drinking during the week. I will drink until I feel the buzz and then stop. No more bouncing checks or lying to get money for drinks. I will only buy alcohol when I can afford it. No more drinking and driving. No more drinking when my son is around, etc.*

The demon inside still tries to pursue any avenue to get what it wants because it knows that it's just a matter of time before you are back into the full swing of substance abuse again.

This is the most challenging part; I can see that clearly. He is 100% correct, that the 95% is the most crucial part. First you must accept the fact that 95% of you needs changing. Then you must master the change process. It's the hardest part of staying clean. The part every addict, at some point in recovery, tries very hard to avoid. *Are you willing to do whatever it takes?*

So a little less than a week into being clean and I know the following; That I cannot change the past, must learn to accept it, repair what can be, and move on. That I must completely overhaul my behavior and change the way I think to secure the present and future. That it will take long term, serious work to stay clean. Reanalyzing and reprocessing Eric James Nekich over and over again until the day he dies. *Are you willing to do whatever it takes?*

16
496 DAYS AND STILL WILLING

I have had some serious ups and downs since my little vacation. I have endured the death of some loved ones, been sued, unemployed, and still to this day I mooch off of my loving sister. I have yet to stand on the ledge of life decisions and wrestle with relapsing. It hasn't occurred to me yet, and I am surprisingly back where I left off twelve some odd years ago. I absolutely loath the stuff. This time for the same reason as the last, *I have had a front row seat to the horrible things it does to people and families.*

To this day I still consider myself in recovery, and hopefully will continue to until the day the good lord calls my number. My relationships with family members and friends have improved vastly. I dream again. I set goals, however small they may be, I set them and accomplish them. I am healing.

I wish I could tell you my secret to sobriety. I wish I had a magic pill for everyone who has, is, or will suffer from this horrible disease. I wish I had some answers for you but I don't. I just gave up giving up. I fought and still fight. *I do whatever it takes.*

Other than that, my journey continues. Eventually I stopped

getting pats on the back and tons of encouragement. Eventually people just accepted the new Eric, or is it the old Eric? He was always there, I just had to do the work to go find him and bring him back to life. I must continue to work to make sure he stays alive.

Not a day goes by where I don't look at that pesky little 95% of me that requires constant monitoring and changing. Always looking inward, always evolving, always changing, and always praying.

I used to pray for God to fix everything that I thought was wrong with my life. *God just get my family off of my ass, God just help me come up with some more money, God don't let the cops bust me tonight!* I am glad God never answered most of those prayers of mine, and answered the prayers my loved ones had for me instead.

Now when I pray I simply say thank you and please. Thanks for one more day of sobriety, love, life, happiness, and simplicity and please, God, let me go just one more day alive, sober, walking in your light, doing *your* will for me.

So, at the end of this story, as I continue to work on my 95% with God, my family and my friends at my side, I really only know one thing for sure. That today I didn't drink. That today I got 5% of my life back. God willing, I'll get 5% back tomorrow, and the next day, and the next day, and the day after that, and the day after that, etc.

Thanks for reading, and if you or a loved one are suffering from an addiction, I will pray, as always, that you get 5% of your life back.

Two new titles coming soon from Eric J. Nekich:

My Dad Used to Drink Beer but Now He Just Drinks Soda All the Time: The Very Basics of Sober Parenting

A humorous look at learning how to parent while learning how to live, clean.

101 Things I Could Have Been Doing, but I Drank Instead

Eric takes a walk down memory lane and recounts the many funny, horrifying, and tragic moments in his life while drinking, and his struggles to seek forgiveness for most of it.